"In the last decade there has been a proliferation of nursery schools and teen-age centers and homes for senior citizens, all of which isolate people at one stage of the journey from people of all others. The Church remains one societal structure that still seeks to reach out inclusively to the whole human family. Why not, then, attempt to describe the topography of the whole human saga — from womb to tomb — so that unique individuals can sense what they do have in common and some of the challenges they can expect, so that what might otherwise surprise them or seem abnormal in isolation can be anticipated and prepared for in advance?"

—JOHN CLAYPOOL

About the author:

JOHN CLAYPOOL is pastor of Northminster
Baptist Church in Jackson, Mississippi, where he
moved from Broadway Baptist Church, Ft. Worth,
Texas. He holds the B.A. from Baylor University
and B.D. and Th.D. from Southern Baptist
Theological Seminary in Louisville, Kentucky.

STAGES

THE ART OF LIVING
THE EXPECTED

JOHN R. CLAYPOOL

A Key-Word Book
Word Books, Publisher
Waco, Texas

First Key-Word edition: June 1980

STAGES
Copyright © 1977 by Word, Incorporated,
Waco, Texas. All rights reserved. No portion of
this book may be reproduced in any form whatsoever,
except for brief quotations in reviews, without
written permission from the publisher.

ISBN 0-8499-4150-4
Library of Congress catalog card number: 77-83316
Printed in the United States of America

To Lue Ann
soul-mate, lover, and friend
in whose company I have journeyed
up and down the mountain and
without whom it would have been
infinitely less

CONTENTS

INTRODUCTION

THE SAGA OF LIFE

Back in 1971, when I became the Senior
Minister of the Broadway Baptist Church
in Fort Worth, Texas, I recall saying to my
colleagues in religious education that I wished
we could pool our insight and sketch out a
road map for the human saga from womb to
tomb. I was fully aware that each individual has
his or her own unique experiences along the
way, but that at the same time there is much

11

commonality in this journey we are taking. The
stages of our lives all follow the same sequential
pattern—infancy, childhood, adolescence,
youth adulthood, middle adulthood and senior
adulthood—and there are many predictable
crises and growth challenges that all human
beings face despite their individual uniquenesses.

I felt it would be of great value to individuals
and to the church in its program formation
to have the benefit of such an overview, because,
contrary to the familiar adage, what we
humans do not know most assuredly can hurt us!
I have seen many individuals caught totally
unprepared for certain situations in life that
seemingly "slipped up on them," particularly
in the largest single segment of life—adulthood.
Dr. C. J. Jung used to emphasize that the
afternoon and evening of life were very different
from the morning; the values and strategies
that apply to the one do not necessarily work
for the others. "Yet where," he asked, "are the
universities to prepare us for the last two-thirds
of our living?" He accurately pointed out that
almost all the emphasis of our educational
institutions is focused on getting people ready

for the morning period of life—enabling them to gain competence, select a vocation, choose a mate, and so forth.

There really is a gap in terms of serious training for the period after forty, and I proposed that the Church was uniquely situated to do something about this vacuum. After all, we are one of the few institutions left in our society that has some kind of contact with all ages of human beings. Not only are we presently divided along racial and social class and ideological lines, but also along generational lines. In the last decade there has been a proliferation of nursery schools and teen-age centers and homes for senior citizens, all of which isolate people at one stage of the journey from people at all others. The Church remains one societal structure that still seeks to reach out inclusively to the whole human family. Why do we not, then, I proposed, attempt to describe the topography of the whole human saga—from womb to tomb—so that unique individuals can sense what they do have in common and some of the challenges they can expect, so that what might otherwise surprise them or seem abnormal in isolation can be anticipated and prepared for in advance?

The idea was greeted with warm enthusiasm, but as so often happens in the everydayness of every day around a big, busy church, nothing was done about it. But four years later, at a winter planning retreat, the idea resurfaced and this time "became flesh and dwelt among us." We decided then to project a month-long church-wide emphasis on "The Saga of Life" in September, when everyone reconvened after the summer. My contributions were to be sermons on the four basic stages of life, one each Sunday morning. In the evenings we would have dialogue with selected specialists in each of these areas, followed by small group workshops with teachers in the various departments of our church school.

The material that makes up this book is the product of that month of emphasis. It has been tested and enriched by interaction with several other church groups—folk from St. John the Divine Episcopal Church of Houston at Laity Lodge in May, 1976; folk from Second

Baptist Church of Lubbock in February, 1977;
participants at the Christian Life Commission
Seminar on "Priorities" in March, 1977; and
folk at the Murfreesboro Baptist Church in
North Carolina. The essence of the content was
shaped for and by the congregation in Fort
Worth in the fall of 1975.

My aim in these sermons was to blend the
light of biblical wisdom with the best from
the behavioral sciences. As a point of focus, I
chose the Old Testament figure David, since
more material is contained in Holy Scripture
about the different phases of his life than of any
other individual, with Moses and Joseph
running a distant second and third. I thought
for a time about using the life experiences
of Jesus as the biblical basis. But the scantiness of
insight into His childhood and adolescence and
the fact that in all probability He did not live
into "senior adulthood" led me to feel the
legendary King of Israel would be a better
resource for this project, though by no means
as supreme an example of full humanity. Those
readers who are versed in the various disciplines
of the behaviorial sciences will quickly

recognize what I have and have not read among the voluminous possibilities there.

It is just as important to know in advance what these chapters are not as well as what they are, for I have found that "disillusionment is most often the child of illusion." Starting out with the wrong set of expectations sets you up for disappointment. These sermons never claimed to be exhaustive or definite statements about childhood, adolescence, adulthood, or agedness. They are, at best, suggestive descriptions of what life is like at each of these junctions, some of the growth-challenges that one can expect to face, and particular resources that the Christian gospel makes available to these situations.

My hopes are modest: first, to provide an individual with perspective on his or her own past, insight into his or her own present, and preparation for his or her own future; and second, to provide an individual some "handles of understanding" into what is going on in the lives of family and friends who are at these various stages along life's way. A veritable explosion of material is coming out now to augment and enlarge these chapters. The fact that Gail Sheehy's volume **Passages** has been a number one best-seller now for weeks is but one sign that our culture is anxious to know more about the afternoon and evening of life and its crises and challenges.

Sam Keene once described a wise person as one "who knows what time it is in his or her life." My highest hope is that some of these words will contribute to the growth of that kind of wisdom.

John R. Claypool

Jackson, Mississippi

CHAPTER
ONE

CHILDHOOD

ANOINTED WITH DELIGHT

For all our individual differences, each one of us begins the saga of our lives in exactly the same way—through the trauma of being separated from a warm and secure place in another's body to having to exist on our own as individuals. At first the condition is one of almost total helplessness and dependency, but gradually two important growth-challenges begin to develop and must be handled either positively or negatively.

The first of these has to do with the issue of personal worth and how the child comes to regard his or her existence in the world. I think it is safe to say that this becomes the number one item on the agenda when a little creature is thrust out of the womb into this new arena. Although the question is certainly not formulated in rational terms, nonetheless the whole organism begins to wonder: "Where am I now? In what kind of context do I find myself? Will my needs be met here as adequately as they were in my mother's womb?" Then comes the most urgent question of all: "How am I regarded in this place? Is it well that I be here? Is my presence valued and welcomed or deplored and resented?" These are the issues that probably dominate the dawning consciousness of a newborn child, and from the very first moment, signals start moving back and forth between "the big people" and the little one that begin to answer the value-question. Every facet of the relationship is significant here—the words that are spoken, the way the child is held, the emotional tone of the whole atmosphere that surrounds this new beginning. Here the process of constructing a self-image begins, and fortunate is the child who encounters positive affection early in life.

Sam Keene was one such child. As he was visiting with his father just before the older man died, he had occasion to look back over their life together and thank his father for the excellent job he had done. "You have always been there whenever any of us children needed you. And across the years, you have given us the best single gift that any parent could give—**you took delight in us.** In all sorts of ways you let us know that you were glad we were here, that we had value in your eyes, that our presence was a joy and not a burden to you."

When I read those words, I recalled something that Gordon Cosby once wrote which surprised me very much at the time. He said that the first and foremost responsibility of any parent was **to enjoy his children!** Given my Puritan heritage, with its emphasis always on the "oughts" and "shoulds," I was startled to hear

the words "enjoy" and "responsibility" in
the same sentence. But, on reflection, I could
not agree more. Nothing can secure a child
more fully in this new world than knowing his
or her personhood brings delight to his parents.

Is not this the way Genesis describes God's
reaction to the creation He had just birthed
into being? He looked at what He had made
and was utterly pleased with it. Things were
far from finished or perfected at that point,
but nonetheless, He who had created all things
took delight in everything He had created.
Such unconditional affection is the foundation
on which all positive self-esteem is built.

But having made that point emphatically,
let me now add two provisos. First, this gift
of delight that is so important must be received
and internalized by the child just as decisively
as it has to be given. There is nothing automatic
or mechanistic here. And the gift of delight
can come from persons other than one's
biological parents. Obviously, the mother and
father are in the best position to give a positive
message to their child, for they have the initial,

foundational contact with him or her, and I am
sure this is God's intention. But even if these
individuals fail, or simply do a poor job, all is
not lost, for the God of the Bible always has a
"backup system" to the primary instrumentalities.
What I am saying is that I believe God will
see that every child is exposed to some form
of delight during those formative years, even
though it may not come through the normal
channels.

This may have been young David's
experience, it seems to me. Over a hundred
pages in the Old Testament tell about this
remarkable human being, but we know less
about his early childhood than any other part
of his life. We do know that he was the youngest
of ten children, having seven brothers and
two sisters, and there are some grounds for
believing that he was hardly a favored child
among them. Do you remember the account
where old Samuel came to Bethlehem and
announced that God had prepared Israel a new
king from among the sons of a certain Jesse
(1 Sam. 16:1–13)? When the father was told
of this possibility, it did not occur to him that

David might be the chosen one. Jesse had
older and more handsome sons than the baby
of the family, and when Samuel asked to see
the members of his family, the older boys were
the ones he presented. Even Samuel was infected
momentarily by this beauty-contest approach
to establishing human worth, but God
challenged that fact by stating: "Humans look
on the outward appearance, but I look on the
heart" (1 Sam. 16:7).

Young David was in fact God's choice, and,
to the amazement of the whole family, he
was called in from the fields and anointed then
and there by Samuel as a person of special
worth and destiny in the eyes of Yahweh. The
important thing to note here is that David,
who had been overlooked by his natural parent,
received this gift of delight when it was offered
him, even though it did not come through the
normal channels. This experience with Samuel
and the Lord God must have helped David to
come to a positive self-image apart from
what his mother and father had done or failed
to do. The Scriptures say that "the Spirit of
the Lord possessed David mightily" (1 Sam.

16:13) through the affirmation of Samuel, and
he was flexible enough to take delight wherever
he could get it and build his life accordingly.

It is important to realize that the task of
helping a child come to a sense of positive
worth does not fall on any one person
exclusively. The parents cannot accomplish
this process all by themselves, no matter how
effectively they love, if the child refuses to
accept and internalize the sense of delight that
is being offered. By the same token, neither can
a child come to a positive opinion about
himself or herself all alone. The sense of delight
must be consciously and deliberately both
given and received. But if there is openness
on all sides, I have faith that God will always find
a person to give the gift of delight to a child—if
not the natural parents, then perhaps an uncle
or a grandparent or a Sunday school teacher
or a friend or someone. It is basic to the
Christian religion that we should always be
willing to do "compensatory work" when the
natural processes of life have broken down.
By the same token, no one has the right to
assume total self-pity or blame his self-despising

27

on the failure of this or that adult. To be sure,
it is a handicap to have parents who cannot or
will not give the gift of delight. But there are
other people around as well, and if one is
flexible enough to receive the gift from whomever
it may come, I believe there will always be a
Samuel to compensate for the failures of the
family.

The words that Jesus heard as He came up
from His baptism are precisely the message
God wants to communicate to every one of
us—"This is My beloved Child, in whom I am
well pleased. This is My Boy, in whom I take
delight" (Matt. 3:17). Getting this message
through and internalized in the depth of being
is the first challenge of childhood. As parents
and friends, we should be diligent to beam
this message as clearly and as widely as we
can. As children, we must be as open and as
flexible as possible to however this gift of
delight might come.

But there is second challenge, and that is
helping children to realize the gifts they have
within them and calling them to become

28

responsible stewards of these powers. As important as a sense of self-worth may be, it is only the first step, for alongside it must come a vision of destiny and a realization that one was created for a purpose and that all one's gifts were meant to become presents for someone else. Thus, a child needs to be given what I call "a Christmas-Tree Spirit" about himself or herself; that is, he needs someone to point out "the packages" that lie all about in one's nature and to encourage him to unwrap and discover and develop these capacities. This had obviously been done for David, perhaps more effectively than self-esteem had been planted. At an early age, he was already out in the fields, involved in the family enterprise.

That something was being expected of David, not just given to him, accounts for his becoming such an outgoing, effective person later on. Early in his life, someone helped David to the realization that he possessed tremendous gifts which were needed by the world and encouraged him to unwrap these gifts and start giving them away. Out of this kind of expectation came the musician, the poet, the athlete, the warrior, the capable ruler who so blessed Israel. Expectation was added to affirmation and acceptance—a combination that helps a child move successfully into life.

Dr. James Dobson has written an excellent little book called **Hide or Seek** on the subject of building authentic self-esteem in our children. In addition to providing them unconditional emotional acceptance, Dobson says that we must help our children recognize their special skills and inspire them to develop them. He feels that our "superstar culture" is very unfair and arbitrary in the way it reserves affirmation for only the exceptionally beautiful and unusually brilliant, but he points out that this is not likely to change overnight. Therefore, we do our children a great disservice if we allow them to grow up without helping them explore themselves and develop some kind of competence that can give them a sense of satisfaction in the world.

Dobson relates his own experience of growing up. Because of his slight physical build, it soon became apparent that he was not going to be able

to compete successfully in football or basketball.
However, his father sensed that tennis was a
game for which he did have aptitude, so he
urged him to learn to play that game. Dobson
said at first he resented having to leave the
sandpile to begin to hit balls back and forth
across a net, but before long his gift began to
emerge and he started finding real satisfaction
in being a good tennis player. Thus, by the
time he got to high school, he had an athletic
skill to compensate for not being able to play
contact sports. This is just one illustration of
how helping our children recognize the powers
that they do possess can aid in the unfolding
of their lives.

In our kind of culture, simply to let them
drift into adolescence without any developed
competence can prove disastrous. I once heard
Charles Campbell of the Federal Correctional
Institute in Fort Worth say that the great
majority of the people in our penal institutions
were not so much bad as they were inept.
Never having developed any skill that enabled
them to function creatively in our society,
they had nothing that gave them satisfaction

or was of worth to the culture. The importance
of this facet of the childhood challenge cannot
be overlooked. No matter how secure a child
may feel in the delight of his family, no matter
how much self-worth may have been internalized,
if he has not also developed a sense of
responsibility to take what has been given
and pass it on to others, then it is not likely
that God's dream for him can ever come true.

Here then, it seems to me, is the nature of
this segment of life called childhood, its unique
challenges, and the Good News of God as it
applies to this point in the journey. The crucial
areas of concern have to do with the issues of
worth and gifts. For parents, the challenges
involve giving the gifts of delight as widely as we
can—to our own children, to be sure, but to all
the children we meet. For children, it means
receiving the gift, however it may come.
Not every biological parent can or will give his
or her children a sense of delight. But God is
not so easily defeated. He has a boundless
reservoir of positive feelings for each one of
us, and if we are flexible and sensitive enough,
He will find some Samuel to anoint us with

"compensatory grace." And there is also the
challenge of expectation to impart to our children
—a sense of responsibility for the gifts they
possess. By the grace of God, they both **are**
something special and can **do** something
special. Expectation without acceptance is a
frightening thing, for it is overly demanding
and becomes a dehumanizing kind of legalism.
But acceptance without expectation is just as
bad, for it leaves unfulfilled the great potential
within a child.

David was blessed by both acceptance and
expectation. He was "anointed with delight"
and made to feel he had something important
to do in history. A magnificent life was built
on these twin foundations. Can we do less
than learn from his example, and in our own
lives, go and do likewise?

CHAPTER
TWO

ADOLESCENCE

THE VALLEY OF TRANSITION

James Dobson has described the segment of the human pilgrimage called adolescence as a "time of indigestion, heartburn and trauma." He says it is hard to tell for whom it is the most difficult—the adolescent who is undergoing all kinds of physical and emotional and social upheavals, or the other members of the family who suddenly realize that this child is not a baby any longer and must now begin on his own to face some of the challenges of life. Dobson concludes that adolescence is a time of life "that offers something painful for everybody."

I think this assessment of things is essentially correct. While every stage of life has its own particular challenges and turbulence, the traumas of adolescence may well be the most intense of all. It is all the more imperative that no one just "happen upon" this period unprepared. The dictum that runs throughout this whole book— **what we do not know most assuredly can hurt us**—is nowhere truer than in that difficult transitional period called adolescence.

Several years ago, while I was pastor in Kentucky, I received through the mail a packet containing a little book entitled **Understanding Womanhood,** together with one of the most poignant letters I have ever read. It came from a couple in the northern part of that state who had only one child—a lovely little girl who was the apple of their eye. They had attempted to give her every material and educational advantage, yet unexpectedly, just as she turned thirteen, she put a gun in her mouth and committed suicide. After her death, they found the diary she had been keeping, and for the first time realized that she had been experiencing great inner turmoil about the changes that were occurring in her body and her feelings and all around her. You see, no one had forewarned her about all the things that start happening to a girl around twelve or thirteen, and the fearfulness of it all was too much for her to handle.

The letter went on to say that the couple had decided to take the money that they had saved up for their child's college education and send a copy of this book to every clergyman in Kentucky. It ended touchingly: "If we had only known and had been able to communicate to our little daughter some of the truths that are in this book, perhaps she would be with us yet."

When I put down the letter, I realized how relevant was Jesus' prayer from the cross: "Father, forgive them, for they know not what they do." Think of the pain that has occurred across the years, not just from human badness, but from human blindness! What those parents, and consequently that little girl, did not know about adolescence did hurt them.

I do not mean to imply that any amount of light will automatically make this segment of the journey easy or painless. However, it cannot but help to know as much as we can about that "valley of the shadows" between childhood and adulthood called adolescence.

The first thing we need to get straight is the meaning of the term itself. The word **adolescence** does not refer to the awakening of sexual awareness in the individual. The technical term for that is puberty. Adolescence stands for the transitional period between the dependency of childhood and the independency—or more accurately, the interdependency—of adulthood. Its length has varied from culture to culture. In many primitive tribes, there was no adolescent period at all. When the time was right, a boy who one day was playing and under the complete control of his parents, would be sent that night on a symbolic hunt; if he survived, he was regarded thereafter as an adult member of the tribe.

40

In our Western industrialized civilizations, however, we have developed the longest period of adolescence in history. It can last for as much as fifteen years in some cases. I know several twenty-six-year-old graduate students who are still being supported by their parents. While they are physically and emotionally adults, in terms of dependency they are still adolescents. Obviously, this is an "in-between" time, a segment of life when an individual is denied the privileges of childhood and yet does not possess the freedom and power of adulthood either.

It is not surprising, therefore, that all kinds of pressures and conflicts surface. In the most literal sense, one encounters "growing pains." Both the adolescent and the family members are faced with something new; that is, they must learn to let a relationship that has existed in one basic form for a decade or so begin to stretch and enlarge without snapping or exploding.

How can the intimacy that human beings have known as parent and child be transformed into the kind of intimacy that is appropriate for adults with adults? This is the challenge that

the period of adolescence flings down before us,
and it takes very different forms for the
various parties involved.

For example, the growth-task facing the
parent is the delicate feat of letting up on the
relationship without letting go of it completely.
The adolescent very much needs for the parent
to step back and give space enough so that he or
she can begin to make decisions on his or her
own. A teenager once complained: "My mother
hovers over me like a helicopter. I'm fifteen
years old, yet if I'm in the basement and sneeze
and she is in the attic, she turns into a distance
runner and is by my side the next moment
saying breathlessly: 'Are you catching a cold?'"
There was a time in that boy's infancy when
such attentiveness was absolutely crucial to his
survival, but now a measure of distance is just as
essential. Not total distance, however—
remember, while the adolescent is no longer a
dependent child, neither is he or she a fully
autonomous or capable adult either. To step back
while not walking out on a relationship altogether
is a delicate feat, and, for the parent, learning

how to distance one's self appropriately from the adolescent is a formidable new growth-challenge.

For the adolescent, the challenge can also be put in terms of distance, but of an utterly different form. He or she must learn to pick up what the parents are laying down, learn to accept responsibility increasingly for his or her own decisions and support, learn the secret of his or her own gifts and the ways of the world, and develop the ability to walk into the larger arena of relationships without walking away from the sources that brought him or her into the world. The goal is not independence so much as interdependency—coming to relate, adult to adult, not only with one's peers, but also with one's parents. Let us repeat the challenges: in the one case, to let up without letting go, to step back without walking out on a relationship; and in the other, to pick up responsibility and walk forward into the world without walking away from one's sources. Nobody ever said it would be easy, and to my knowledge no family or person has ever carried

it off perfectly—not even King David,
remarkable human being that he was.

The whole seventeenth chapter of 1 Samuel
describes a climactic moment in the drama
of David's adolescence. He was obviously at an
in-between stage. He was no longer playing in
the sandpile out back, but rather was out in the
fields tending sheep. However, he was still
under the control of other adults—his father
and subsequently Saul the King. Three of his
brothers had enlisted with Saul to fight the
Philistines, and one day David's father suggested
that David take them some food and bring
back word of their welfare.

When David arrived at the battle station, he
was dismayed to find the forces of Israel
quaking in fear. A huge mountain of a man
named Goliath came out from the other side
every morning and evening and challenged any
Hebrew to engage in one-to-one combat.
There had been a day when Saul the King would
have risen to such a challenge in a moment,
but his courage and confidence had left him, and

44

as a result, the whole Hebrew army was
being unmanned with fear.

David's reaction was a classic expression of
adolescent idealism. He came into that situation
unjaded and unfatigued by life, which is one
of the great roles that youths play in the process
of history. He had not "been everywhere and seen
everything and done it all." He had an
exuberant faith in the God of Israel and great
confidence in his own abilities. Thus, to
everyone's amazement, this shepherd boy
offered to accept Goliath's challenge and fight
for the honor of the Lord of Hosts!

When word of this boldness got back to Saul,
he sent for the young man. What follows is a
classic interaction between an emerging
adolescent and the older generation. Saul's first
reaction was surprise; it startled him that a lad
who so shortly before had been playing
underfoot would now be making "man-noises"
and proposing to do something significant.
(It is easy to freeze our children sentimentally
in the baby category, so that almost invariably

their emergence as significant individuals catches us by surprise.) David countered the charge that he was merely a child by telling of having fought lions and bears out in the wilds as a shepherd, until finally it dawned on Saul that the one before him was not a baby any longer, but a young man come of age.

Saul's next reaction was also typical. Realizing David meant business and was ready to go out and fight Goliath, he proceeded to load him down with his own armor—to take the shields and breastplates that had been designed for him and put them on David. This must have been a comical spectacle indeed. Saul was reputedly a very large man, standing head and shoulders above the average Hebrew. Just imagine how young David must have looked in all that oversized get-up. He could not even move, much less fight. Yet is not this precisely what we parents do when it finally hits us that our children are going to have to move on unaccompanied by us? Don't we hurriedly try to dress them up in our ideas, our advice about this and that, what we did on our first date or in high school or so forth?

What we do not realize is that they are unique individuals living in a different time from our past; somebody else's armor does not fit nor is it really what they need. Every person must forge his or her own weapons and beliefs and convictions.

In speaking of children in **The Prophet,** Kahlil Gibran very wisely says to parents: "You may give them your love, but not your thoughts, for they have their own thoughts. You may house their bodies, but not their souls, for their souls dwell in the house of tomorrow, which you cannot visit, not even in your dreams. You may strive to be like them, but seek not to make them like you, for life goes not backwards nor tarries with yesterday. You are the bow from which your children as living arrows are sent forth. The Archer sees the mark upon the path of the Infinite, and He bends you with His might that His arrows may go swift and far. Let your bending in the Archer's hand be for gladness, for even as He loves the arrow that flies, so He loves the bow that is stable." This is so true, and David reminded Saul of that as politely as he could.

47

History is not a treadmill, nor is one individual a carbon copy of another. We can give our children a certain feel for life, a sense of what is right and wrong. We can "train them up in the way they should go;" that is, we can point them in the right direction, but when it comes to the specific armor they will need, it is not our sacred responsibility, but theirs, to fit themselves out with it.

David had obviously done his adolescent growth-work rather thoroughly before this moment. For example, religion was not a secondhand tradition as far as he was concerned. He had obviously come to terms very personally with Yahweh. He had moved from the "what-I've-been-taught" stage to the "what-I-believe" stage, and this only occurs when one is encouraged "to ask and to seek and to knock." If we adults fall in a faint the first time a teenager expresses doubt or begins to search, we hinder the very processes that lead eventually to mature faith. This is a point where "letting up" on indoctrination and stepping back to make room for growth is essential.

David had also begun to know himself—he

48

recognized the shape of his individuality and its boundaries. He had tested his skills in the give-and-take of life. Long before this moment, his parents had begun to remove their protective shell and allowed him to go to work and face the wilds of the desert. In that process he had come to understand something of what the world out there was like and how he himself was equipped to cope with it. Thus, in that moment before the King, David did what every adolescent has to do—he took responsibility for his own life and asked for the right to meet a challenge with his own resources and ingenuity.

Here is the climactic moment in the high drama of adolescence—the point at which the young person has the courage "to leave father and mother" and walk forward on his own toward the giant called life, and the parents have the courage to let the beloved one go with only the sling and staff of his own choosing. It is hard to say which of these two challenges requires the most courage. It is certainly not easy for any of those involved. Just imagine what must have been going through David's mind as he stepped out there alone before that nine-and-a-half-foot monster. And how must Saul

and David's brothers have felt as they
watched David move into that ravine?

"The valley of the shadows of adolescence" is
scary, but we might as well face the fact that
there is no way around it! David never could
have become the adult he became apart from
this kind of experience. All parties concerned
functioned well in this moment, and it became a
building block for the legendary career that
was to follow. The relationship between David
and his sources stretched and expanded that
day without snapping or exploding. The intimacy
appropriate to childhood grew into a different
kind of intimacy—that of an interdependent
adult with adults. David had the courage to take
the responsibility for his own existence from
his parents, but as he walked forward into
the world, he did not walk away from a
continuing relationship with his sources. He
remembered that he was able to see as far as he
could because he was standing on the shoulders
and the accomplishments of his sources.

By the same token, his parents and Saul had
the courage to let up without letting go of

David altogether. They stepped back at the
appropriate time, but they did not walk out on
the relationship completely. This is essential,
for adolescence is not one dramatic experience
never to be repeated once it is over. Most of the
time it involves a series of forays into the
world from which one then comes back wounded
and bleeding, in need of healing and reassurance.

Not every adolescent does as well against
the giants of the world as David did. Jesus told
once of a younger son whose decision to launch
out on his own proved disastrous (Luke 15:11–24).
Unlike David, this young man had not done
his homework: he did not know himself or the
world, and he wound up losing everything
in the far country. His first reaction was to run
home and try to climb back into the womb.
He had had his fill of freedom. What he wanted
now was the security of being a hired servant, of
having someone else make all the decisions
for him. Luckily for him, the father who had let
up and stepped back had not let go or walked
out on his son completely. When the lad
came limping home, defeated by life, the father
refused to let him reenter dependency. He

showed him great compassion, but then called
for a robe and a ring and some shoes to
symbolize the adulthood to which this son was
called. In other words, the father's parenting
responsibility continued long after the adolescent
left for the first time, and this is how it should be.

Alan Paton summarized the stance of the
parent beautifully in these words: "I see my son
wearing long trousers; I tremble at this. I see
he goes forward confidently, he does not know
so fully his own gentleness. Go forward,
eager and reverent child. See here, I begin to
take my hands away from you. I shall see
you walk carelessly on the edge of the precipice,
but if you wish, you shall hear no word come
out of me. My whole soul will be sick with
apprehension, but I shall not disobey you. Life
sees you coming, she sees you come with
assurance toward her. She lies in wait for you.
She cannot but hurt you. Yet go forward.
Go forward. I hold the bandages and the
ointment ready. And if you would go elsewhere
and lie alone with your wounds, I shall not
intrude upon you. If you would seek the help of
some other person, I will not come forcing

myself upon you. If you should fall into sin, innocent one, that is the way of this pilgrimage. Struggle against it, not for one fraction of a moment concede its dominion. It will occasion you grief and sorrow, it will torment you. But hate not God, nor turn from Him in shame or self-reproach. He has seen many such, and His compassion is as great as His creation. Be tempted and fall and return. Return and be tempted and fall, a thouand times a thousand, even to a thousand thousand. For out of this tribulation there comes a peace, deep in the soul and surer than any dream."

And that, in the end, is the hope that illumines this valley of transition called adolescence. "Out of this tribulation" can come a peace, a wholeness, a magnificent human being like David. As James Dobson pointed out, there is something painful for everybody in this time of indigestion, heartburn, and trauma. But it can be endured; "yea, the valley of the shadow of adolescence" can be walked **through** to the light on the other side! But let us not forget that in order to do so, everybody involved faces a challenge. For the parents, it is learning to let up without letting go, to step back without walking out on the relationship. For the adolescent it is learning to pick up what is being laid down, and to walk forward without walking away from one's sources. Stretching and expanding a relationship so that everything becomes bigger, without snapping or exploding the bond—this is the challenge adolescence poses for us all. May God give us courage, like David's long ago, to face into this particular challenge, and by His grace, grow on through.

So let it be!

CHAPTER
THREE

ADULTHOOD

UP AND DOWN THE MOUNTAIN

I sometimes wish I had never heard that
familiar formula that comes at the climax of so
many fairy tales: "And they lived happily
ever after." As a rule, everything leading up to
these words is colored by conflict and struggle.
Dragons have to be fought, curses broken,
and all kinds of effort exerted. But then suddenly,
out of all the world, Prince Charming and
Sleeping Beauty find each other, and the

atmosphere changes radically. It is like coming out of a choppy sea into an utterly tranquil port, for the rest of life is described in that idyllic image—"and they lived happily ever after."

The reason I am sorry I heard so much about this as a child is that it distorted my expectations of what adulthood was going to be like. It gave me the illusion that the "morning of life" was the time of turbulence, and that once a person had finished his or her education, chosen a vocation, selected a mate, and settled down, all would be serene and placid thereafter. The hassles of having to grow and change and decide were supposedly all behind a person at that point. However, the truth of the matter is that nothing could be further from actual experience. These six words really are a fairy tale in the most literal sense. Think of the people who have been crippled with disappointment and disillusionment because they thought adulthood was going to be one kind of experience and it turned out to be another!

I would have been far better off if I had gotten my "feel for life" from the Bible rather

than fairy tales, for God's Book never fosters
the illusion that life gets easy at some point or
that the challenge to grow comes to an end.
Jesus said: "In the world, you shall have
tribulation" (John 16:33). He did not restrict
this statement to childhood or adolescence; it is a
description of the whole human pilgrimage.
Such realism is not to be confused with
pessimism, however. Jesus went on to say:
"Be of good cheer; I have overcome the world."
He means that, while He does not promise to
deliver us **out** of tribulation and struggle and the
need to grow, He will show us how to cope
with all this and will enable us to be "more
than conquerors" of our circumstances rather
than conquered by them.

As we turn now to the largest single segment
of the human journey—adulthood—this is
the point I want to underline. It is not the time
of life when automatically and effortlessly we
begin to "live happily ever after." Both in terms
of pressures and possibilities, it is the most
strenuous segment of our existence. If
adolescence is the most **intense** stage along the
way, I would say adulthood is the most

demanding. Not only is it so long, it also involves so many different challenges simultaneously. Gail Sheehy has coined the phrase "concomitant growth" to describe the unique challenge of adulthood, and I believe she is correct. It means continuing to grow concurrently on the three basic frontiers of adulthood: work or vocation, relationships with one's "significant others," and one's own unique selfhood. Let's face it— this is quite a challenge indeed. Have you ever known an adult who handled all of it perfectly?

The great temptation here is to become unbalanced, to give the vast majority of one's energies to only one of these areas and neglect the other two. Gail Sheehy tells of a forty-six-year-old TV newscaster who had climbed to the top of his profession and was basking in the affluence and affirmation that went with being a national celebrity. However, he was not as satisfied or fulfilled as one might suppose. He commented one day: "I am near the top of the mountain that I saw as a young man, but lo and behold, this is not snow up here, it is mostly salt." He said most of the persons he knew who were considered "successful" had

left their personal lives far behind them.
Professionally, they were terrific, but on a
personal level their lives were in utter disarray.
What has happened, he notes, is that these
individuals quit growing relationally and
personally somewhere between the ages of twelve
and fourteen when the crying ambition to
succeed overwhelmed them, but now that they
are looking out from "the top of the heap,"
a whole new agenda emerges.

Going down the mountain is quite a different
art from climbing up it. Where, asked that
celebrity, are the navigational charts for descent,
the kinds of relationships that will sustain a
person in the afternoon and evening of life?
This is a classic example of what happens to
someone who has worked on only one growth
front during much of his or her adulthood. This
man was feeling great loneliness and personal
emptiness because work and concern with
succeeding professionally had dominated his
whole existence.

Failure at "concomitant growth" may
sound like a twentieth-century phenomenon,

but it is not: three thousand years ago, David
did the very same thing with his adulthood,
and the consequences which resulted from such
imbalance were mixed, to say the least.

On the one hand, like that TV newscaster,
David "made it big" professionally. In fact, it
was incredible how in five short decades he
rose from the obscurity of tending sheep to
be the uncontested ruler from the Nile to the
Euphrates. Such success was attributable to
many factors, of course, but basic to it all was
David's remarkable ability to concentrate
on doing something rather than just being
something.

I shall never forget the time I first heard that
distinction drawn. A personnel manager of a
national firm said this was the thing he tried to
determine initially about any new executive
trainee. He described the person who wanted
to be something as one whose ego needs
were still dominant in his or her existence.
Thus, at every juncture, this one would be
asking: "How can I use this situation to enhance
my personhood and position?" This kind of

person, he said, "will always have blurred vision, will never be able to risk anything or sacrifice, and thus would be a liability in the higher echelons of decision-making. However, the person who wants essentially 'to do something' had his or her ego needs met healthily. This one can look at a difficult situation with a single eye and ask simply: 'What needs to be done here?' This kind of person can risk and sacrifice, and will be worth millions more to the company throughout his or her career than the person who always strives 'to be something.' "

Now the secret to David's great professional success lies right at this point—he was consistently the kind of person who wanted to do something rather than be something. He did not have to waste energy bolstering his own ego or acting spitefully. Getting on with the task of making Israel a great nation was foremost on his agenda, and again and again this priority enabled him to do the strategic thing.

For example, King Saul treated David most unfairly for many years. David was never

anything but a loyal and helpful subject, but
the king's insecurity led him to harass David
unmercifully. Yet when Saul and his son were
killed in battle, David did not rub his hands
together and gleefully say: "It serves the old
scoundrel right." With all of Israel, David went
into genuine mourning. Eventually, this lack
of vindictiveness led the northern tribes who
were close to Saul to ask David to rule them as
well. When this happened, David made another
strategic move. He could have made his
headquarters in Hebron the new capital, and
thus ground into the tribes of the north that he
had won out over them, but this would have
been an ego trip for his benefit alone, not a
move to unify the country. So instead, David
conquered a Jebusite stronghold called
Jerusalem that the Israelites had never
controlled before and made this neutral site
the center of his new beginnings.

This was David's greatest strength—he
had moved from the infantile need to have
everything serve him to the maturity of
genuinely wanting to serve others. Psychologists

identify this attitude as one of the
distinguishing marks of maturity: the point
at which we cease to be preoccupied with what
parent-figures can do for us and decide to
become parent-figures and mentors ourselves,
that is, to care for and bless and guide other
people. Erik Erikson calls it "generativity,"
and without it no person really comes to the
fulfillment of life. All of us start out in utter
dependence, but woe unto us if that is where
we remain all of our days! This does not mean
everyone must have a career or engage in
some professional activity, but it does mean that
in our adulthood, some way, somehow, we
should become part of the answer instead of
part of the problem and contribute something
positive to the stream of history.

David is a real model for us at the point of
generativity and of making a difference in
the world by giving himself. This aspect of his
life was great. The problem was that there was
not concomitant growth on the other frontiers
at the same time. For when we turn to a
consideration of the rest of his life, it becomes

evident that David's overinvestment in the area of work led to tragic neglect in the other facets of his existence.

Take, for example, the area of family or significant other persons. If an individual is determined to be a workaholic, as David turned out to be, it appears that he or she would choose not to take on the responsibilities of establishing personal intimacy. Tragically enough, this is rarely the case. More often than not, people like David involve themselves heavily in these ways, and then create wastelands of neglect. For example, it does not appear that David ever worked through one of the primary tasks of adulthood; namely, establishing a relation of authentic intimacy with another person. He had many wives but no deep relationships, and as a result he grew lonelier and lonelier as the years went by. It is much easier to substitute several superficial relationships for the task of building one master-relationship in life, but the outcome is not the same. Infected by our trade-in, throw-away mentality, the TV newscaster I mentioned earlier had gone from wife to wife in his climb up the ladder. Every time this man and his mate encountered difficulty, instead of using the occasion to deepen and strengthen their bond, he slid off sidewise and established another superficial alliance.

From what we can tell in 1 and 2 Samuel, this is what David did as well, and he encountered the inevitable end of that pattern of relating— utter and awesome loneliness. The TV celebrity really wanted some companionship as he started down the mountain, but the way he had used his relational powers held little promise. By his own admission, he had never put much of himself into that side of life, and as the Bible says: "He who soweth sparingly shall reap sparingly" (2 Cor. 9:6). David came up short in the same way, and he grew lonelier and lonelier and lonelier.

There is something for us all to learn here: it takes genuine effort and persistence to establish an intimate relationship with anyone. Neither good marriages nor, for that matter, even deep friendships are made in heaven. They may be designed there, but the work of constructing them is done on earth, and only those who are willing to stay with the long-range task of faithful relationship-building will avoid the loneliness that was recognized long ago as not good for any human being.

David's failure in the area of intimacy includes his relationships with his children as well. He had lots of them, to be sure; the Bible lists at least nineteen sons and no telling how many daughters. From the way they later fought and connived and betrayed each other, it seems clear that from the beginning they had little contact with or guidance from their famous father. To use Gail Sheehy's term, there was no concomitant growth on the relational frontier of David's life. He zoomed way out in professional competence, but at the expense of the people closest to him. And I imagine, as David looked back over his life from the perspective of old age, this particular overinvestment and neglect caused him no little pain.

It is also fairly obvious from the record that David put forth very little effort in cultivating his own inwardness and uniqueness as a person. Lewis Sherrill says that while preoccupation with self is a weakness in adolescents, it becomes an essential task in adulthood, for developing a coherent view of life and coming to terms with the uniqueness of one's individuality are so important. Oscar Wilde once wrote, "It is tragic how few people ever possess their own souls before they die. 'Nothing is more rare in any man,' says Emerson, 'than an act of his own.' It is quite true. Most people are other people. Their thoughts are someone else's opinions. Their lives are a mimicry and their passions a quotation."

I have seen person after person let someone else decide everything for them for so long that when you ask them: "What would **you** like to do?" they have no answer. Having been programmed externally for so long, they have no earthly idea. Do you realize that more suicides occur on Saturday and Sunday than all the other days of the week put together? The reason for this "week-end psychosis" is clear. When life has been structured by someone else all week and suddenly the individual is left to decide things for himself, many are so unskilled in "listening to their innermost thoughts" and answering the voice of their uniqueness that they crumble under the pressure.

One spring David did not go to battle as he had been doing for years and years. With the structure of external habits removed, he did not know what to do with himself. And it was during such a period that he saw Bathsheba from his roof top and set in motion a train of events that proved disastrous for all concerned.

The cultivation and care of one's own inwardness is utterly important lest we grow old in great emptiness. When Jesus challenged His disciples to "bear much fruit," this is part of what He meant—to get in touch with all that is within us and begin to bring forth the treasures of that uniqueness. As we have seen, David had done a better job of growing outwardly than inwardly. He had neglected the cultivation of his own individuality, and the result was sad indeed.

The challenge, then, is to concomitant growth, simultaneous development in the spheres of work and relationship and selfhood. Herein lie

the great growth-challenges of adulthood—
generativity, intimacy, and self-fulfillment. And,
I repeat, this is by no means an easy task for
anyone. Not even David—legendary figure that
he was—managed to achieve this balance. Like so
many before and after him, he overinvested
himself in work to the exclusion of family
relations or personal self-realization. I have
known others to get just as much out of balance
by overinvesting in family life or "doing their
own thing" to the exclusion of work. One thing
is obvious—real life is not like the fairy tales.
There are no points beyond which struggle and
growth are not called for.

We will live happily ever after only to the
degree that we take the ideal of concomitant
growth seriously and keep on working all our
days at the tasks of generativity, intimacy, and
self-realization. To exclude any one of these leads
to distortion and incompleteness. For most
adults, this is a forty-year enterprise. May God
help us not to waste a single day or leave out
any one of these important tasks!

CHAPTER
FOUR

SENIOR ADULTHOOD

FOCUS ON BEING

This chapter marks the last leg of an important journey. Our original intention was to attempt to sketch out a road map of this human pilgrimage in which we all find ourselves. What is it like to be a child, an adolescent, an adult, and finally an aged person? For all of our individual uniquenesses, there are certain predictable characteristics and challenges in each of these segments, and our underlying

assumption has been "the more light, the better."
Here again, as we have found earlier, what we
do not know most assuredly can hurt us!

At no point in this process have I attempted
to hold myself up as an expert in these matters.
I am as much a learner and a fellow struggler
in this way as any of you. However, I must
confess that I am less comfortable at this juncture
of our study than at any other point, for the
obvious reason that I am dealing with something
that I have not yet experienced firsthand. Up
to now, I have had at least some existential
knowledge to go on, for I have experienced
what it is like to be a child and an adolescent
and a young and median adult, but I have not
yet experienced the phenomenon of agedness. I
do not really know firsthand what it feels like
to have your physical powers diminish or to
retire from work or to see an increasing number
of your contemporaries pass away into the
mystery of death. Therefore, I want to
acknowledge this limitation at the outset and
confess that I write as an outside observer.

Let me also acknowledge, however, that I
have been fortunate in having some great mentors

along the way in this area. My work has given me the opportunity to share deeply with lots of people as they negotiate "the evening of life." My own parents are now in their mid-eighties and I have learned volumes from watching the way they have aged with grace. Then too, I have been most blessed to have served as a colleague with Dr. Franklin Segler during my days at Broadway Church. He has taught me much about this period of life, both through the fine little book he has written on the subject and, more importantly, by the way he himself is handling this stage of life so creatively.

Another factor to be noted here is that senior adulthood or agedness is not all that unconnected with the stages of life about which I do know something. At the same time, I am not denying the special dimension of uniqueness of this stage. In terms of what happens to one physically and vocationally and relationally, this time of life represents "new ground" and poses a full set of brand-new growth-challenges. However, the other side of that coin is that we are preparing all through our lives for the time of agedness, whether we realize that fact or not.

One of the main lessons I have learned from this study is the vast interconnectedness of life. The way a person handles the challenges at one period of his or her existence directly affects all that is to follow. Thus, in a very real sense, we begin laying the foundations for our agedness as far back as childhood, and the segment of life we are talking about now represents the culmination of how well or how poorly we have done our growth-work at earlier stages. I do not want to be misunderstood here: I firmly believe that genuine change is possibly at every stage along the way of life. It is never too late nor is one ever too old to alter radically the shape of one's existence. Still, the truth of the matter is that what we become in agedness is a culmination of the choices and habits we have developed in childhood and adolescence and adulthood.

This was certainly the case with King David, the man whose life saga we have been studying throughout this journey. I was interested to find two distinctly different accounts of the last stage of David's life. In 1 Chronicles (29:26–28) there is a later, rather idealized version of this

period. The great religious piety of David is
emphasized, and one would assume from this
account that the final hours and the transition
of power from David to Solomon were easy and
automatic.

In 1 Kings, however, a very different picture
is painted. The kinds of struggle that had
characterized all of David's reign continued.
For example, it was by no means simple to settle
the issue of succession. (It never is when great
wealth and power is involved.) Absalom had
been "the apple of his father's eye." As David's
first-born son he was the logical heir to the
throne, but, as you may remember, Absalom did
not know how to wait. Reaching for the crown
prematurely, he tried to take by force what
would have eventually been given to him, and
in the battle that ensued, he was killed. Later,
when it became evident that David was very
weak and about to die, Adonijah, the next son
chronologically, did the same thing Absalom
had done. Traveling to the northern section of
Israel, he proclaimed himself as the king and
attempted to take the crown from his father's
head. He was joined in this effort by Joab, the

head of the military establishment, and Abiathar, the high priest and leader of the Temple.

No sooner did this happen, however, than the prophet Nathan stepped into the power struggle. He was the one, remember, who had stood up to David years before concerning his treatment of Bathsheba and Uriah the Hittite. Now he apprised the aged king of what was happening and reminded him of a promise he had made Bathsheba in light of the pain he had brought into her life. The child conceived of their initial affair had died, but later on, after Bathsheba had become David's wife, she had borne him another son named Solomon. This was the child to succeed David, in Nathan's judgment, for Solomon, who never had been a warrior like his father, had a brilliant mind and was obviously the best equipped of all David's children to do the things that needed to be done next in the Kingdom of Israel. David acted with the same sagacity that had characterized the decision-making of his life, announcing his choice and counseling Solomon to eliminate Joab and Abiathar immediately to solidify his ascendancy. I do not mean to imply that this last action was particularly admirable, but it was strategic;

the point I am making is that David in his
agedness was the culmination of what he had been
becoming across the years.

There is an awesome interconnectedness to
the various stages of life. What we are to be in
the future we are now becoming, which means
that agedness is not as remote and unrelated
as we might think just because we are twenty
or thirty or forty. While it is true I have not
yet experienced senior adulthood, I am
nonetheless preparing for it right now in the
way I live and grow. One of the points that
Dr. Segler emphasizes in his book is that we do
not wait until we are sixty-five to begin to get
ready for agedness. All of life is a preparation
for the final and climactic act, so it is never
too soon to begin to get ready for this stage.

But exactly what is the unique challenge in
"the evening" or final stages of life? In his famous
essay, "The Eight Ages of Man," Erik Erikson
defines this last growth-challenge as achieving
"ego-integrity." And just what does he mean
by this rather abstract term? I think he is talking
about achieving a positive and hopeful

perspective about three things—about one's own personhood, about one's life, and about one's death. The concept could also be described as a coming to a sense of peace and satisfaction about one's worth, one's past, and one's future. When you stop and think about it, are not these qualities the mirror opposites of despair? What is that dark state, if not the feeling that one's personhood has no worth, that one's past is a bleak failure, and that the future holds nothing of promise to which to look forward? Coming to the opposite of such conclusions— that is, being able to bless one's self in terms of personhood and past and future—is what "ego-integrity" is all about. Dag Hammarskjöld said: "For all that has been, thanks! For all that will be, yes!" The person who can join him wholeheartedly in that statement has come to the pinnacle of human maturity, and in the terms of the Psalmist, has so numbered his days that he has gained a heart of wisdom (Ps. 90:12).

But how, practically speaking, does one go about achieving such a mature perspective on life? What can we begin doing, here and now, so that we shall be able to feel such positive things about the entirety of our existence?

At this point the Christian gospel can be extraordinarily useful indeed, for it speaks of **grace** and **providence** and **hope,** and these realities are uniquely related to the issues of self and past and future. For example, the answer to the question of personal worth can be found in an understanding of God's grace. This is the secret of true security and self-esteem. Once, in a group of which I was a part, the leader asked each one of us: "What is the most important single thing about you? What are you depending on the most when you die and stand before your Maker? Is it your family name, or your accomplishments, or your possessions or what?" That kind of probing was very revealing to me, for I came to see that anything less than the grace of God would not be sufficient in such a moment.

In the final analysis, it is what God has made of us, not what we have made of ourselves, that is our hope. And the way to prepare for a positive perspective on self at the end is to begin now to ground our lives and hopes in the reality of grace, not in works. Saint Paul said: "By the grace of God, I am what I am." This realization stands us in good stead in the evening of life.

Paul Tournier observes that agedness is that time of life when the focus of living shifts from doing and having to being. Quite often a senior citizen does not have the strength or opportunity to do as he once did, nor does the possession of certain things seem that important. After all, if one is bedridden and almost blind, what difference does it make if there is a Jaguar sedan in the driveway or a hundred suits in the closet? As life at this stage focuses down to the reality of being, how satisfying it is to know that one's worth comes ultimately from the love God has for us, rather than from what we do or have or can earn. To have settled early in life that it is by grace we are saved, not by works, is the best preparation I know for the positive self-perspective so essential to the evening of life. The waters of grace will support our whole weight if we can learn to trust them. Happy is the person who does not wait until he is sixty-five to discover the basis of such self-esteem.

The second thing in the gospel that contributes to this kind of perspective is what I call providence, or the belief that life is destiny and not just a process of blind chance. This means coming to believe that in all things God has been at work for good. It is not just the pleasures and the triumphs that bear the mark of God's hand, but all events—the bad as well as the good. Real maturity is achieved when the bittersweet quality of all existence is accepted rather than resented. "All sunshine makes a desert," states an old Arab proverb; wise is the person who comes to realize this fact and begins to acknowledge hardship as "the elder brother of good."

A young woman reminiscing about her youthful days once wrote: "I loved my uncle's ranch when I was a child! There was space to run unhampered, freedom to explore. The dust lay inches thick upon the trails, and running barefoot down the path of sifting powder was a

sumptuous sort of feeling. The barn was my
playground, full of animated toys. In the loft
there were hay and mice and fairly friendly
spiders. The mint grew wild and plush beside
the creek, and my aunt made berry pies and the
smell would seek me out wherever I played
around the house. I rode my cousin's palomino
horse through fantasies that never seemed to
end. If I am not careful, Lord, I can edit out
these memories and forget that I got a bee sting
where I picked the mint and burned my tongue
time and time again on the berry pies because
I never seemed to learn and couldn't wait. Or
that the barn smelled just awful or that the
horse made my bottom sore and the dust that
felt like sifted powder made me sneeze all
summer. If I'm not careful, I can forget all these
things. But if I'm wise, I will remember that
all of life has both of these things in it."

It is very important that we never conclude
that only the pleasant and the beautiful have
positive value. The truth of the matter is that
life is a bittersweet reality, and that is its
essence and its glory. For the final outcome both
the sunshine and the shadows are needed.

A belief in providence, in a God who is at
work in all things for good, can lead to that
perspective on the past that enables one to say:
"For all that has been, thanks!" It is one thing
to look back and say: "For **some** of what has
been, thanks!" To embrace all of life in that
thanksgiving is something quite different, but it
is the perspective that a belief in God's goodness
and wisdom provides. Understanding life as
destiny, not happenstance, and acknowledging
God's hand as having been **in it all**, does make
for gratitude and acceptance and the ability to
end one's days at peace with the past.

One further gospel reality is involved here, and
that is the power of hope—the ability to look
toward the future and even toward death with
positive expectancy. Reuel Howe tells of visiting
with an old friend who was nearing death. The
man, fully aware of his condition, said quite
calmly, "You know, I am amazed at how all this
is working out. I had always wondered what
it was going to be like to die, but lo and behold,
it is not all that unusual. Death has turned out
to be an old acquaintance in different garb."
He went on to say, "For years now, I have

undergone experiences like this. From my earliest days, I had to learn to let go of some things that I had in order to get some of the things I did not have. This is what I did the day I started to school or left home to go to work or launched out on a new career. It turns out I have died a thousand deaths across the years, and in all of this I have learned something: **every exit is also an entrance!** You never leave one place without being given another. There is always new life on the other side of the door, and this is my faith as far as death is concerned. I have walked this way before. Death is an exit, to be sure, but at the same time, it is also an entrance."

I cannot think of a finer image of hope than linking "exit" and "entrance" together. The way this man came to such hope is significant as well. As he said, the last challenge of life is not so different from what we face again and again in our pilgrimage. Beginning in earliest childhood, we do have to die to smaller worlds if we are to reach bigger ones, and in every case, there is life on the other side of those crises of risk and growth. No exit ever leads us out to nowhere. Every exit is also an entrance, and learning this fact is what gives a person hope and the ability to say: "For all that will be, yes!"

This is what I think Erik Erikson means by the phrase **ego-integrity** as over against despair. The final challenge of our earthly existence is coming to a positive and hopeful perspective about ourselves, about our past, and about our future. And how can we do this? The Gospel offers three indispensable resources: grace, providence and hope. It enables us to say three things: First, "By the grace of God, I am what I am." That statement speaks to the issue of self-worth. Secondly, "For all that has been, thanks!" That statement speaks to the past. And finally, "For all that will be, yes!" That statement speaks to the future. This is what "ego-integrity" is all about, and from the account in 1 Chronicles, it appears that David achieved this goal, for we are told: "He died in a good old age, full of days, riches and honor" (29:28).

And the truth of the matter is that you and I can do the very same thing. The time to begin to prepare for that kind of ending is right now. It involves learning to ground our whole

existence in the grace of God. It involves coming
to believe that life is destiny, and that in all
things—the bitter and the sweet—God is at work
for good. It involves learning through a thousand
little deaths and resurrections that every exit
is also an entrance.

Isn't it time, then, to learn of grace, to learn
of providence, to learn of hope? Right here is
the secret, not just of good living, but of good
dying as well.

Well, what are we waiting for—?

PERSONAL STORIES
OF FAITH

BEST-SELLING
KEY-WORD PAPERBACKS
BY KEITH MILLER
& BRUCE LARSON

☐ 91036   **THE BECOMERS,** Keith Miller $1.75
Your first step toward becoming all God created you to be . . . learn how to communicate and establish goals.

☐ 4111-3   **THE TASTE OF NEW WINE,** Keith Miller $1.75
In this classic bestseller, Miller opens up his personal life—his doubts, failures, hopes, and prejudices—to declare his faith in a personal God who cares. A milestone book of honesty, uncluttered by cliches.

☐ 91015   **A SECOND TOUCH,** Keith Miller $2.75
Here's real hope that in the midst of frustration, loneliness and anxiety the power of a Christian lifestyle can overcome.

☐ 91012   **THE ONE AND ONLY YOU,** Bruce Larson $1.50
Unleash your God-given uniqueness and live a liberated life that claims God's gifts of hope and giving.

☐ 4107-5   **ASK ME TO DANCE,** Bruce Larson $1.95
Helps you find new ways to look into your heart and the hearts of others in your search for the joy of becoming whole . . . to realize that there *is* life after rebirth in Christ . . . that it's O.K. to feel deeply and express your feelings.

☐ 91010   **HABITATION OF DRAGONS,** Keith Miller $1.75
Become a dragon-slayer today as you conquer your personal problems with the power of prayer.

HELP YOURSELF WITH
KEY-WORD BOOKS

KEY-WORD PAPERBACKS
HELP YOU GROW!

☐ 4127-X **PRAYER AND YOU,** Cecil G. Osborne $2.95
Offers insights on many aspects of prayer; how your relationship
with your human father affects your feelings about God; how anger
can be as valid a part of prayer as adoration; answered and
unanswered prayer; guilt, forgiveness and prayer.

☐ 91033 **RELEASE FROM FEAR AND ANXIETY,** Cecil G. Osborne $1.75
Means and methods for securing your own liberation from fears
and anxieties that plague everyone.

☐ 91022 **YOU'RE IN CHARGE,** Cecil G. Osborne $1.75
A close look at man's internal conflict between his desire to be free
and his reluctance to accept responsibility for his actions.

☐ 91030 **THE GIFT OF INNER HEALING,** Ruth Carter Stapleton $1.75
Discover the healing therapy of creative faith imagination in this
case-book look at dealing with deep hurts and wrong attitudes.

☐ 4125-3 **ANY CHRISTIAN CAN,** Douglas Elliott $2.95
A personal guide to individual ministry. Here are clues to discov-
ering "hidden" opportunities all around you for helping others. It
teaches the most effective ways for you to open up relationships
and keep them growing.

Buy them at your local bookstore or use this handy coupon for ordering:

KEY-WORD BOOKS   P.O. Box 1790, Waco, Texas 76703

Please send me the books I have checked above. I enclose $_____ (please add 75¢ for the
first book and 25¢ for each additional book to cover postage and handling), in check or money
order—no cash or C.O.D.'s. Please allow 4 to 5 weeks for delivery.

Mr./Mrs./Miss _____

Address _____

City_____ State/Zip_____

KW-3B

MARRIAGE & FAMILY BOOKS FROM KEY-WORD

☐ 91031 **THOROUGHLY MARRIED**, Dennis Guernsey $2.50
Help for Christian couples who are seeking to break through to an honest, open, free relationship.

☐ 4100-8 **PARABLES FOR PARENTS AND OTHER ORIGINAL SINNERS**, Tom Mullen $1.50
There's a lot of wisdom mixed into these 30 rib-tickling reflections on parenthood.

☐ 4130-X **AFTER THE WEDDING**, Philip Yancey $2.95
Nine couples tell how they survived the most dangerous years of marriage. Positive, realistic, and helpful, particularly for newlyweds.

☐ 91023 **FUN AND GAMES IN MARRIAGE**, Dorothy T. Samuel $1.50
A priceless collection of ways in which love can be kept alive and growing in a marriage.

☐ 4121-0 **WHERE TWO OR THREE ARE GATHERED TOGETHER, SOMEONE SPILLS HIS MILK**, Tom Mullen $2.50
"I spill milk. You spill milk. All God's children spill milk, and when we learn how universal this experience is, we'll be able to move beyond crying over it." Give yourself a laugh by reading this very clever, funny book.

☐ 4105-9 **BIRTHDAYS, HOLIDAYS AND OTHER DISASTERS**, Tom Mullen $1.95
A witty, somewhat irreverent look at the delightful little things that make up your life.

☐ 91019 **HAPPINESS IS STILL HOME MADE**, Cecil T. Myers $1.75
Here are tested principles for turning "daylight and dishes" into "moonlight and roses" all marriage long.

☐ 4152-0 **PARENT ALONE**, Suzanne Stewart $2.95
After eight years of marriage, Suzanne Stewart's husband told her and their three children to move out. This is the story of her heartbreaks and hardships, and how her faith has helped her to cope.

☐ 90029 **IS YOUR FAMILY TURNED ON?**, Charlie W. Shedd $1.25
For families concerned about drug abuse and the way it is destroying American homes, here is Dr. Shedd's helpful guide for coping and prevention.

Buy them at your local bookstore or use this handy coupon for ordering:

KEY-WORD BOOKS   P.O. Box 1790, Waco, Texas 76703

Please send me the books I have checked above. I enclose $_____ (please add 75¢ for the first book and 25¢ for each additional book to cover postage and handling), in check or money order—no cash or C.O.D.'s. Please allow 4 to 5 weeks for delivery.

Mr./Mrs./Miss _____

Address _____

City _____ State/Zip_____

KW-5

KEY-WORD FAVORITES

☐ 4111-3 **THE TASTE OF NEW WINE, Keith Miller** $1.75
In this classic bestseller, Miller opens up his personal life—his doubts, failures, hopes, and prejudices—to declare his faith in a personal God who cares. A milestone book of honesty, uncluttered by cliches.

☐ 4119-9 **HOW TO BE BORN AGAIN, Billy Graham** $2.25
"I have wanted to say everything that was necessary to help people who really want to know God," says Billy Graham. He cuts through the morass of theological argument to reveal a direct, real approach to Christian conversion.

☐ 4118-0 **PLEASE LOVE ME, Keith Miller** $2.50
A sensitive chronicle of one woman's search for love, acceptance, and the miracle of intimacy. Miller's true story of a remarkable woman.

☐ 91014 **THE STORK IS DEAD, Charlie Shedd** $1.50
Your teenager will find wise advice on sex and judgment in this frank, honest look at the 'whos', 'whats', 'whens' and 'whethers' of sex.

☐ 4103-2 **THE FAT IS IN YOUR HEAD, Charlie Shedd** $2.25
If every diet in the world hasn't moved your belt in one notch then discover the cure in your soul through a special relationship with God.

☐ 91016 **STAUBACH: FIRST DOWN, LIFETIME TO GO,**
Roger Staubach $2.95
The Dallas Cowboy quarterback tells it all in a book of humor and human interest, tragedy and triumph.

☐ 91026 **AIN'T GOD GOOD, Jerry Clower** $1.75
A bestseller that unveils the fascinating life history of comedian Jerry Clower.

☐ 4137-7 **THE HELPER, Catherine Marshall** $2.25
Catherine Marshall's 40 devotional helps have touched the lives of more than 400,000 readers.

Buy them at your local bookstore or use this handy coupon for ordering:

KEY-WORD BOOKS P.O. Box 1790, Waco, Texas 76703

Please send me the books I have checked above. I enclose $_____ (please add 75¢ for the first book and 25¢ for each additional book to cover postage and handling), in check or money order—no cash or C.O.D.'s. Please allow 4 to 5 weeks for delivery.

Mr./Mrs./Miss _____

Address _____

City_____State/Zip_____

KW-1